The Diary
of a
Young German Soldier
1917 - 1918

The Diary
of a
Young German Soldier
1917 - 1918

Edwin Valentine Kühns

1899 - 1996

Translated by his wife, Joyce Kühns

AVON BOOKS

1 Dovedale Studios
465 Battersea Park Road
London SW11 4LR

Printed and bound in the U.K.

Avon Books

London
First Published 1998
© Edwin Kühns, 1998
ISBN 1 86033 591 8

In Memory of
Edwin Valentine Kühns
1899 - 1996
and
All the Servicemen and women who
gave their lives in both World Wars.

PHOTOGRAPHIC
ACKNOWLEDGEMENTS

The photographs on pages 30, 32, 33, 34 and 35 (bottom of page) are reproduced by the courtesy of Orbis Books from the book "World War I in Photographs" by Adrian Gilbert, photographs on page 36 by the courtesy of Arms and Armour Press from the book "A Photohistory of World War I" by Philip J. Haythornthwaite and photograph on page 31 (Q29950) by the courtesy of the Trustees of the Imperial War Museum, London.

PREFACE

Edwin Valentine Kühns was born 14th February, 1899, in Kolonie Brinsk, Rural District of Strasburg in West Prussia. Later the family moved to Thorn (Polish Torùn) on the river Vistula (Weichsel) where his father was a clerk in the County Court and where they remained until 1945 when his father died.

He was educated at the local schools and entered the Teachers' Training College in Thorn. It was in his first year, in 1917, that he was called up, at the age of 18 years, as a Reservist in the Telephone Section in W.W.1., on the Western Front in the Arras-Cambrai Sector.

West Prussia is a region of rolling landscape with farms and pine forests. The family had never travelled further than Danzig and Posen, so it was a great experience for a young fellow to be responsible for leading a group of four other recruits, all older than himself, to find their Division on the Western Front. All this is reflected in the very detailed accounts of the landscape, villages and towns that they passed through and later their surroundings and daily routine on the Front Line.

There are moving accounts of how he visited his father serving in another area 60Km away and how his small group celebrated Christmas and New Year under such primitive conditions. There are also descriptions of experiencing his first bombardment and seeing the first immobilised English tank.

At one point they were situated near Bourlon Wood and until recently, he had the dried pressed violets that he had gathered there. From the higher ground of Bourlon Hill, they were able to see the big tank battle of Cambrai in 1917.

The retreat of the German soldiers is also recorded with the same detail, the return to his family in Thorn and the resumption of studies at the Teachers' Training College - a story very much with a beginning and an end.

Rather than a day to day entry, it is a narrative written at intervals, whenever time was available, in fine Gothic handwriting. At times, this has been difficult to decipher, but at the time of writing this he is able to recall, at the age of 97 years and with poor eyesight, many of these incidents and the comrades mentioned.

Joyce Kuhns
January, 1996

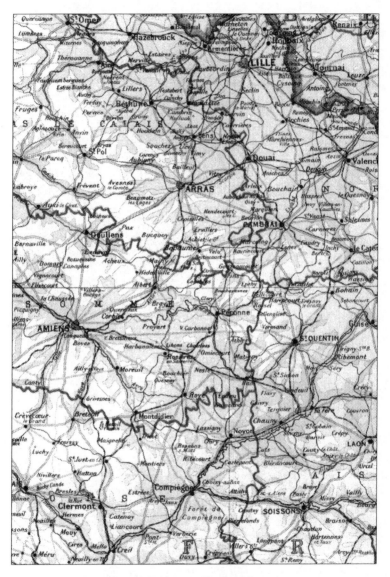

Map of the Arras - Cambrai Sector.

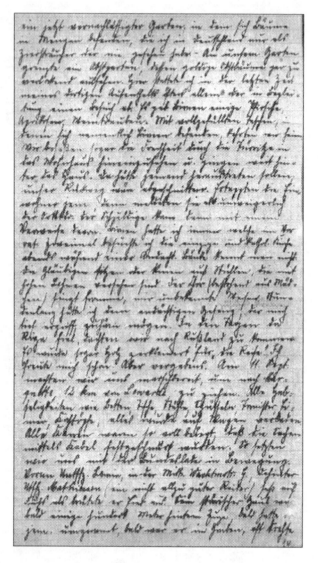

Above and opposite:
Pages from the original diary, the English translation of which
is housed in the archives of The Imperial War Museum.

ARMY RANKS
ABBREVIATIONS & TRANSLATIONS

General	Gen.	General
Hauptmann	Hauptm.	Captain
Leutnant	Ltn.	Lieutenant
Wachtmeister	Wachtm.	Sergeant Major, Technical Divisions
Vize Wachtmeister	Vize Wachtm.	Subordinate. Often older, long-serving Regular Soldier
Feldwebel	Feldwebel	Sergeant Major, Infantry
Unterofficier	Untffr.	Corporal
Gefreiter	Gefr.	Lance-Corporal
Stations Ältester		Senior N.C.O. from Regular Army

The Diary
of a
Young German Soldier

June 15th, 1917, marked the arrival of my call-up papers to the Infantry Regiment 141 in Memel and shortly afterwards, a second to the Telephone Reserve, Division 5.

On 26th July, 1917, I was drafted to the Telephone Reserve Division 5 in Hammerstein (West Prussia) and on the same afternoon we left Thorn Station under the leadership of Vize Wachtm. Markons and Gefr. Bredon.

Awaiting me at the station were Mama, my sister Stefka and brother Leonard. With a handshake and kisses we said our farewells and it was with a heavy heart that I left my home town, all my friends and my loving family.

The whistle blew and slowly the train began to move. I looked out of the window and waved. The last houses became smaller and smaller until Thorn, my much loved native town, disappeared over the horizon. The journey went via Kulmsee, Graudenz, Konitz, Tuchel and Schlachan. In Kulmsee, I was able to say farewell to Aunt Pelagia and my cousins and received the first gifts which consisted of cherries, raspberry juice, smoked fish, lemons and filled rolls.

After several hours of waiting at all the main stations - in Konitz from 10-3.30 a.m. (I slept on the luggage rack) - we arrived by special train (one engine and one carriage) at Hammerstein at 4.30 a.m. I was taken aback when I saw green trees, meadows and barracks made of stone. I had imagined the camp like a sandy desert with wooden Army huts, like most military camps.

After two days of being put into groups and being kitted out, we began our first duties. Here I would like to mention Vize Wachtm. Jantzen who put us through our paces. It was a nuisance having to have numerous injections; between 30th June and 13th July. In a stable, on 20th July, our group, both Catholic and Protestant, took its oaths supervised by a Protestant priest. After that, we had our free time until 10 p.m.

Just at this time, dysentery broke out in the camp because of the contaminated food. I went down with it as well on 22nd July - headache and stomach pains, loss of appetite and exhaustion.

Twice, with my friend Jeziovski, from Thorn, Fischerstr., we went into the forests of Pommerania. There, we found a stone surrounded by Juniper bushes, with the inscription "Here 7.8.15 Franz Kretchmer of the Territorial Army 3,K.3.Saxony T.A. Battalion XII murdered by a Russian P.O.W."

On 1st August, we went down to the Rifle Range. 1 shot from the standing position, in a sitting position and with the rifle supported. Result: 3.11.9. For this I used two different rifles hence the rise and fall in the result. On 28th July, there was a huge fire in the town. Fanned by the wind, it spread quickly and engulfed five buildings. Most of the soldiers and our group too, were given the alarm at 5 a.m. I found myself very near to the fire on the roof of a three storey house and when I got back I was blackened from all the smoke.

Our training lasted from between 6½ to 8 weeks. We were woken at 4 a.m. From 6-8 a.m. drill, 8.30-11 a.m. technical subjects and Morse code, 11-2 p.m. lunch break and then further lessons until 6 p.m. Quite often we had to march 8-10 km. with the Cable Construction group. The technical subjects were very boring. When one had been sitting on a hard chair from 8.30 - 11 a.m. without a break and has had to listen to the monotonous voice of the instructor, then quite often the eyelids closed and one dropped off to sleep, especially when the subject was of little interest. For example, the last three days were about the crank movement. When, at the end of the lesson, the order came "Chair in the hand, right turn and march to the lecture room!" one heard, "What a boring session! Now I am off to have a long sleep!"

On 10ᵗʰ August, the first recruits went off to the Front. They chose 50, including Jeziovski from Thorn, Fischerstr., transferring them to the Reserve Company and then the next day, they were despatched to the Front. Jeziovski, with four others, came to Kowno. He wrote that he had a switchboard with 25 stops and only 4 hours duty.

On 15ᵗʰ August, on the Rifle Range. First round lying down, result: 10.8.9. At the end of the shooting, Hauptm. Weber, Ltn. Van der Heyde, his Feldwebel, and Ltn. Peitchker came to the Range. Hauptm. Weber shot in a standing position 0.0.2! The Ltn. was not much better. Hauptm. W. gave orders for the three best shots to come forward. After repeated calls from Watchm. Jantzen, I volunteered and two other recruits followed suit. Kneeling, I took aim. 3 shots at a Ring Target at a distance of 200m. Result: 7.8.9. The next one shot 6.0.3. and the last one 3.0.0. The last also hit the nail on the head! From Hauptm. W. I received a commendation and a note in his lists. Watchm. J. was delighted and recommended a spell of leave. This was returned to Wachtm. J. with the remark, "Leave it until later." Jantzen then invited me to his room and offered me a good 25Pf. cigar!

During mid-August, most of the recruits moved out to the Fronts, namely Western, Eastern, Romanian, Turkey, Macedonia etc. The others and I, who were in the choir, were given more time. I was also in the football team for a long time. We had very smart black uniforms with white collars in which I felt very proud. I had my football boots repaired and paid for by the Company and then sent them back home.

Due to the new grouping a new Tel. Operator - Walter Baum from the Teachers' Training College, 2ⁿᵈ Year, in Eschwege near Kassel, living in Limburg on the R.Lahn - shared my room. He was three years older than I was (16.8.1897). We struck up a close friendship and he later became (until he died at the age of 81 years, added by translator) my best friend. I admired him for his command of literature. As a parting gift, he gave me his photograph and the book *Der Reiter auf dem Regenbogen. (The Rider on the Rainbow)* by Storm; with the message, "To my dear friend, Edwin." He was very depressed when he was transferred to the Telephone Tapping Corps. For me too it was soul destroying. As I left for the Front, I gave him my photograph - *Memories of Thorn* - and my visiting card, for which he thanked me very much.

On the day of my departure, 27.8., from Hammerstein 1.39 p.m., my mother left for home, having visited me twice. Worried about my future, she left with a heavy heart and tears in her eyes.

On further demand from the Reserve Company, another 50 recruits were drafted. Because of a longing to go to the Front, over the last few days, I was included. It was now 30th August. The next day, we were handed our grey uniform and I was proud to be wearing the grey uniform of a soldier of King Friederick. The next day we were divided into groups. Vize Watchm.J. allowed me, the student teacher Volze, from Kassel and the student Paul Rohr, from Zoppot, Seesteg 3. to stay together. He granted us our wish and drafted us to the Telephone Division 1047 which was supposed to be in Arras.

On 25.8. I, having been appointed as leader of the group, was given the surety that we would have to leave on 28.8. That morning, I was given all the necessary equipment, such as rifles, rations (3 loaves per man, 2 tins of meat, money in lieu of rations 2M, refreshments 3.5M) and distributed them to the group. I had decided that we should assemble to march to the station at 5 p.m. A short time before this, the heavens opened and it poured with rain but we had to go. There was a short farewell to all our comrades and with heavy knapsacks, we three telegraphic operators and two drivers (of horses) who I had to take as well, set off for the station. Walter Baum carried the wooden trunk for me. Soon, the train arrived. We got into the special compartment and left Hammerstein at 6.15 p.m. on 27.8.1917.

We looked back at the town for a long time which had housed the camp where we had been for the last 8 weeks. I had been given the exact timetable and route which we had to travel as far as Olpaden, near Cologne but I did not take it too seriously. In Konitz, where we should have waited from 9 p.m. to midnight, I told them not to get out and so we arrived in Berlin at 5 a.m. at the Schlesische Station. I asked for bread ration cards (200gr, per man) and put forward the suggestion that we should tour the city, which was unanimously agreed. After we had put our packs in the luggage office and had just a bag for bread and the tinned meat, we went into the city and bought a town plan.

We visited the Royal Palace, Parliament Buildings and part of the town. Then we went up the *Siegessaule* (Victory Column) where 192 steps took us up to the first platform where the column was decorated with mosaics. Another 54 steps brought us to the top which was surrounded and enclosed by an iron grill. From there we had a wonderful view of the surroundings - the Country's capital lay at out feet. Just below was the statue of Hindenburg, the Parliament Buildings, the *Sigesallee*, the Brandenburg Tor, with its statue of Victory. After this, we went down again and lay in the park, where in a quiet corner, with a hearty appetite, we ate our bread, tinned meat and drank coffee. My suggestion to visit the Maritime Museum was turned down. On the way to the Royal Palace, we visited the *Zeughaus* (War Museum).

On the ground floor were models of French towns. As well as this were uniforms of soldiers from the time of the great

Electors to the present time. There was also the splendid ship's cannon presented to the Kaiser by Krupp van Bohlan Halbach. His Royal Highness had it put in the War Museum. On the opposite side of the entrance, in glass cases, are models of the zeppelin Parcefal, airships and aeroplanes. Going into the Courtyard, in the background, visitors are aware of an aeroplane, the aeroplane of Air Ace Boelkes. Nearby are German and enemy shells. In the hall on the right are a number of cannons - old ones from the time of the Electors, of which one was used in *Grossfriederichsburg* (Gold Coast) and nine from this World War.

In the room where Boelkes' aeroplane stood are German, French, Belgian and English machine-guns. When one goes upstairs, there is another room hung with paintings of the war. Next door, in another room, are weapons and guns. Of historic interest is the car of Major Hills, the hat and sword of Napoleon and Blücher etc.

As it was now lunch-time, we went to a *Gasthaus* and ordered beer, coffee and soup and ate our own bread. Then we went to the Underground station to reach the Zoological Gardens. The carriages, both first and second-class, looked like electric trams. We only stayed a short time as our departure was imminent. We left Lehrten Station at 7.18 p.m. and passed through Rathenow at 9.30 p.m. I was anxious to see the Elbe Bridge but fell asleep and woke at 2.40 a.m., shortly before we pulled into Hanover. Here we had to wait one hour, during which I asked the Red Cross to provide each of our men with 200gr. of bread.

At dawn, 5.36 a.m. we arrived in Minden. Here, according to our timetable, we should catch the special Army train at 7.05 a.m. We all got out and I went and asked the Station Master for information. He said that the special train had been cancelled and that we should continue in this train. Now we had to get in again with our packs. Hardly had the last door slammed, when the train started moving. There was a lot of swearing and cursing and the train and Station Master could go to the Devil!

Then came Herford at 7 a.m. and then Bielefeld. Here we passed Kochs Adler's Sewing-machine factory. Now we travelled through the Porta Westfalica and in front of us flowed the R.Weser. The Weser hills rose steeply on either side and in the distance, on top of a single hill, whose slope was thickly forested was the Kyffhauser Monument. We watched this for a long time until it vanished out of sight. Shortly afterwards we were surrounded by the high hills of the Teutoburger Forest which is famous in German history. In a desperate battle, Armin or Herman, the Gherus prince, conquered the Romans in 1 A.D. After this, came the towns of Gütersloh (Railway Junction), Hamm, then Unna, Dortmund.

From here I wanted to go direct to Cologne but my friend, Volze, asked if we could go via Düsseldorf. He had arranged by telephone, that his girlfriend, at the Girls' Lyceum (Grammar School), should meet him there. I let him have his wish. We travelled through the Ruhr industrial area with coal mines everywhere, one next to the other. Almost the whole way we went through towns. At noon on 29.9., we arrived at Düsseldorf. Volze talked and thought only about his sweetheart. He was overjoyed to see her on the platform. Rohr and I were introduced and we talked for a short time and then I gave him permission to go off until our train was due to leave at 5 p.m.

First of all, the five of us put our packs in the luggage office and then went to the Red Cross for a meal. For 30Pf. we had a large portion of lentils and meat which everyone enjoyed. A young Red Cross nurse came and sat with us and told us about all the sights worth seeing. We travelled by tram to the Market and left the tram shortly before the Rhine Bridge. We bought plums and pears and looked up at the Rhine Bridge and the Father of Rivers itself. At Düsseldorf it is about the same width as the Vistula in Thorn (Torùn) but the water is much clearer as the gradient is much steeper. There were lots of lovely paddle-steamers on the river and near the bridge is a church with an extraordinary leaning spire. On the way to the town, we saw a lake with boats, so we went for a boating session for forty minutes. This lake, with an island in the middle, was in front of the Art Gallery. Travelling on the tram, we noticed that it ran almost silently compared to the trams in Thorn. The most beautiful street in Düsseldorf is the *Konigsalle* which is also the main street and the town itself made a better impression than Berlin.

About 5 p.m., we left Düsseldorf and were in Cologne by 9.30 p.m. In the twilight, we saw the huge cathedral, as we passed, in some places, above the town. Before we actually came to Cologne itself, we came to the collecting point at Opladen Station. Up to this point, our timetable was planned so we all got out and were given a warm meal. Now we had to travel by the Army Transport train with an Officer's deputy in charge of the troops.

After the train started, I went to sleep and woke up on the Thursday morning as we passed through Aachen into the Belgian countryside. On either side, there were gentle grassy slopes and hills clothed in bushes. We often had to go through long tunnels and little towns which had been partly destroyed. Then came Verviers, Liège, Leuven and Brussels. Everywhere I bought postcards and took them as souvenirs, for the future, of past times. All the stations are covered with huge roofs and one sees lots of factories such as the Ruisbrock Sunlight Soap factory in Brussels. Near Brussels is the canal where we saw numerous Belgian rectangular barges pulled by horses. Just behind Tournai, we saw a huge building, probably a monastery as it was joined to a church, with a huge red cross. It was now probably a Field Hospital.

Thursday evening 8.45 p.m., after passing Tournai, at Blandain, 3Km. from the French frontier, we heard the first gunfire from the Front and flashes in the sky. With Hurrah Germany! we crossed the Franco-Belgian frontier. On Friday, just after 1 a.m., we arrived in Douai, via Lille, where we were given sleeping quarters in the Rupprect Barracks formerly "École des Beaux-Arts, d'Industrie et du Commerce" and "École Nat. de Musique". Here we ate breakfast for the first time in a French town!

Now began the search for our Unit. Firstly, we were sent back to Lille. From here we were sent by tram to just before Quesnay, which was 5Km. behind the Front. At the terminus, I learnt from a Feldwebel and Untffr. that Q. was totally destroyed, so we had to go back to Lille. Rohr made two bad mistakes: a) he left his rifle in the tram and a man came along with it and b) when we got to Lille, Rohr wasn't there - he had missed the train, so I had to get out at the Clearing Office and wait for him. In Lille, we were given sleeping quarters for the night - in a very large *Gasthaus* called 'Silvana'. We looked round the town and saw the Grand Place and *Hôtel de Ville* which had come under fire. The town itself, especially around the station, was in ruins. We went to a restaurant called 'Zum Feldgrauen (Grey Uniformed), once *Cafépalast.* Before we turned in for the night, we were startled by gunfire. We rushed outside. It was an enemy aircraft being shot at by the anti-aircraft guns.

The next day, Saturday, we asked for dinner at the station and set off for Douai. The whereabouts of our Unit was not ascertainable. We should go to Marquette where our Army Postal Service 408 was stationed. By chance, I met a soldier from the Teleph. Corps 1047 who gave us the right directions, so we started off towards our township Lewarde - 6Km. south of Douai, Ikm. behind the Front. Here we were greeted warmly by our comrades who were leaning out of the windows. We had then to go to the Office where I had to make a report to

Wachtm. Gunther: One transport leader, two Teleph. Operators, two Drivers (horses) ordered from the Reserve Tel. Unit 17 to the Unit 1047. Thereupon, I handed him a report which had been given to me in a sealed envelope.

After a short inspection by the Wachtm., we were dismissed and went to quarters which were allocated to us. The Tel. Operators had a whole flat which had once been occupied by a pensioner. We were seven men to one room. Our accommodation comprised of wooden bunks, with wood wool as mattresses, covered by a groundsheet; on top, we used our blankets and trenchcoats. We three "new boys" were put onto receiving long-distance calls on the telephone. This apparatus was in a small room, the windows of which looked towards the Market Place. Here, I often used to look out of the windows and saw columns of soldiers who came here for a few days' rest. Very few telegrams arrived and the hours of duty were long, for example, Mondays 8 a.m.-1 p.m., night watch 1 p.m.-8 a.m. On the same day 8-10 p.m., Wednesdays 1 p.m.-8 p.m., Thursdays 8 a.m.-1 p.m. etc. To alleviate the boredom, I read letters, newspapers or caught up with my letter writing. During the night duty, I occupied myself until midnight or 1-2 a.m. then we took it in turns to sleep. I usually slept first, and then Untffr. Matthieson, Stations Ältester. The first time, when we had been given orders and I was ordered to do it myself, I occupied myself and slept alternately.

During the day, when I had free time, I lay, when it was good weather, on top of a 2 ½ m. high garden wall. A small lime-tree spread is leafy crown over the wall and gave some welcome shade. A blanket was spread out, a pillow put in its place and I either read or had a short nap. When Rohr was there, he either recited or read poems. It was unpleasant to be indoors, because Wachtm. Gunther used to come and then he gave us other jobs to do. The cookhouse was in a nearby house. At first, I enjoyed the food but as we ate cabbage 4-5 times a week, I didn't want to eat it anymore. Every day, we had a good portion of meat, also barley, semolina and even stewed steak! Potatoes were bought by the group and everyone paid 20-40Pf. Every third day, we received our rations. We took our tins, boxes, jars and grease-proof paper to the cookhouse and were issued with 4 cigars, 4 cigarettes, 105grm. lump sugar, tobacco, jam, margarine, butter, cheese and 1800grm. bread.

A large neglected garden belonged to the house with a number of flowering bushes and trees that I had never seen in Germany. Next to it was an orchard with tempting ripe fruit. During the last few weeks, I had often been over, either alone or with company. There were pears, some peaches, apricots and grapes. We came back with bulging pockets, mostly with pears. We were daring enough to look through the cracks in the door and went further behind the house. Someone came out of the house so our way back was cut off. If the people living there caught someone, then it was reported to the Commanding Officer. The guilty ones were given a severe reprimand but I always had pears in store!

Twice, I went to the evening Service in the Catholic Church. They don't have pews. The worshippers sit or kneel on chairs with high backs. The choir, all girls, sang music unknown to me, but I could have listened for hours.

When the town of Riga fell, we thought that we would have to go to Russia. Even the firewood was chopped for the stoves on the journey. I thought it would be wonderful but for nothing. On 11th September, we made ourselves ready for the march to Marquette, 12Km. from Lewarde. All our possessions, such as chairs, tables, basins, knapsacks, buckets, and saucepans, were loaded onto wagons. They were all so full that they had to be secured with ropes. So we set off with all our baggage. In front was Untffr. Mattiessen (not a very good rider) mounted on *Fuchs* (Fox) like a broody hen on eggs. His wild horse was already a few hundred yards behind the troops. Very soon he ran into someone, then he was in the ditch and kept running round and round and outwitted his rider. The Wachtm. rode here, there and shouted commands. In the meantime, it looked as though the wagon would tip over or some of the baggage fall out. When the wagon went round a corner, it had to be supported. Anyway, we arrived safely in Marquette after a three hour march (5 p.m. to 8 p.m.) Marquette has 2,300 inhabitants and lies in a hollow, so that, except for the church spire, we cannot see it from where we are stationed.

The village was bare except for a few orchards. The Wachtm. put us in more or less satisfactory quarters. Gefr. Kern, Telephone Operators George, Zabel and I were billeted in 8 Rue Abacon. It was a primitive little house at the entrance to the village. The beds were like those in the Rupprect Barracks in Douai; a wooden bunk with mesh wire and wood-wood on top. Over that I put my "Hero's Coffin" (groundsheet), my small straw sack which I had brought with me and my pillow. As a cover, I used my jacket and trenchcoat. Rohr and Kern soon started complaining that the wood shavings were dropping onto their faces. So we all had to get out of bed and change everything round for the sake of everyone's health and comfort. The next day, Kern brought sacks filled with straw.

At 7 a.m. the next day, we had to fall in line and start our new duties. With Zabel, I had to lay light and telephone cables. As a novice, I stood there and watched but then the officer in charge (Master builder) found me another job, cleaning the walls. Just my luck!

On the second day, 13.9., George and I were ordered to go to Aniche (1 was to learn how to operate the Field Exchange). I sat there for two days and then, after our Unit had been rearranged, Volze and I were put on duty. Here there was as little work to do as in Lewarde. While on duty, I occupied my time reading and writing up my diary. Duties are from 8 a.m.- 1 p.m., 5-9 p.m. Next day only one: 5-9 p.m., etc.

Billeted alone, my room is an attic with a window in the roof the size of an A4 sheet of paper which lets in enough fresh air. For me, the prize piece is my bed. It is wide enough for two, even three, people to sleep in it comfortably. Underneath is first a sack filled with straw, above one with sea-grass and then a feather bed, covered with a white sheet. Over this is a blanket in a white duvet cover. As it is often quite cold in the early morning, I have my own blanket as well. What I don't like is the long, hard bolster. The other bits of furniture are a round table, two chairs, two rugs and a crucifix -sparse but comfortable. My belongings take up one wall. The lady of the house and her daughter are nice, friendly people. Quite often they spoil me with luxuries and extra treats such as fruit, sugar and bottled fruit. Twice for supper she cooked potatoes, which are in short supply here, in the traditional way - baked in hot sand or ashes. Madame sees to bedmaking and cleaning my room and even doing my washing. She lends me plates and cutlery which she washes up - in every way very kind. Through installing electric light, my room is much more comfortable and I don't have to swallow down my supper by candle-light.

Here in Aniche, as in other villages which are 15-20Km. behind the Front, there is little to be seen of the fighting and the inhabitants are all still there. On Sundays, everyone goes out for a walk and the "beauties" try to make contact with the soldiers because, after all, we are good looking chaps! But cavaliers, who admire pretty little feet, are disappointed as there is a prevalence of flat feet like the farmers' labourers in West Prussia. There are, however, very pretty girls who match up well to those back home. Enough! Otherwise I shall be blamed when I get back to Germany.

I often thought that I might not stay here long so I sometimes went to Douai on the tram. Twice, I was unlucky when I missed the last tram back and a section of the cars took one and a half hours to get back at 11.30 p.m. I would have liked to have stayed in Aniche but one day rumour had it that we were having to leave, on 30th September. The provisions wagon took part of our belongings to Marquette and on 1st October our group of 6 men was driven in a private car to Oisey le Verger, via Arleux.

I must recount one of my experiences - an air attack on 30th September, 10.10 p.m. It was the first bombardment that I had experienced. There was a wonderful full moon when I came back at 9 p.m. and switched on the electric light and had my supper. It was really too pleasant to turn in for the night, so I decided to use the time for writing up my diary. I had written several lines when I heard a humming like an approaching tram but soon it came nearer and nearer and became louder. Curious, I went to the little window in the sloping roof and saw to my right, very low to the ground, what I thought was a German 'plane. It looked magnificent in the moonlight, as it floated in the sky. I couldn't see the English markings because of the bright moonlight. Then suddenly, about 80m. away, there was a terrific bang, then a shudder and all was quiet again. Shortly after came another and then I realised that it was an enemy aircraft. In a flash, I turned off the light and went down to the cellar. In the dark, I went downstairs while the bombs were falling. Madame and her daughter rushed out from the kitchen, the latter saying that, in her opinion, she had seen a German 'plane from the window. I urged Madame: *"Nous allons dans la cave"*. There was then machine-gun fire. Soon the noise stopped and the planes, possibly 3 or 4, flew away. One flew round for some time, so I went out onto the street to verify that the air was clear of the 'plane, and then went to bed.

To all Madame's friends, who all liked us very much, we said our farewells and left Aniche at 9 a.m. After a short drive via Monchencourt, Fressain, Aubigny au Bec, Aubenchieul, crossing the Douai-Cambrai road and passing the lakes near Arleux, we arrived in Oisey le Verger. The village has 1,800 inhabitants and lies 25Km. S.E. Arras, 13Km S. Douai, 10Km.

N.W. Cambrai. In the road triangle A.C.D. the distance between Arras and Cambrai is 42Km, between Arras and Douai 23Km, and between Douai and Cambrai 23Km. Oisey lies near the Cambrai to Douai Road.

Duties started the same day but no one bothered about sleeping quarters. I had to sleep the night on the floor where we had our switchboard. The next day, we moved into a house which was next door. We are four to a room and the windows look out onto the Market Square. Here, we have a wonderful view of a beautiful Romanesque church and a section of the Front. Everything has been rebuilt. There is a Reading Room, Field Bookshop and cinema - so near to the Front! - which I went to the evening we arrived.

On 2nd October, I received the sad news that one of our good friends from the same class had been killed, behind the Front, as they were practising with hand-grenades. Dobrint was also killed in the middle of September this year. Rumour has it that we may have to be transferred to the Infantry. Happy thought! Now a second lot of training with the *Sandhasen* (Sand hares i.e. Infantry). I am thinking of volunteering to train as a pilot in a flying squadron.

For a whole week, there had been no sighting of an enemy aircraft. The evenings are so dark that you can hardly see your hand in front of your face. The cold season has already begun. On Sunday, 7th October, there was rain mixed with snow and in the morning there is frost on the roofs.

24.10 From self-determination, I am learning shorthand, system Stolze Schrey. My teacher, Volze, is very earnest but the pupil takes it lightly. Harsh words are exchanged as the one that learns pits his brains against the teacher. I am still in difficulty moneywise because the number of pieces of soap that I send home have to be paid for. The *Kaiser* (pay-out every ten days) is eagerly awaited.

Our area belonged to the Departement Artois. During my

few walks, I came to a hillock on the outskirts of the village, which is cut across by trenches 10m. deep. Further on were the most beautiful lakes and ponds surrounded by a belt of poplars. On the edges there are rushes and a narrow path and such clear water that one can see the bottom of the pond and the reflections of the surrounding vegetation - away from everywhere and so quiet and so beautiful. If this were my home, I would be here every day. The soil that I have seen here is loamy with patches of clay and very fertile. Because of this I think it is responsible for the huge size of the swedes and carrots that we often have to peel for meals. Some of the swedes are about 8lb. each, the carrots are as thick as an arm and one and a half hand spans long.

At school, in the psychology lessons, we learnt that everything that was one-sided was not a good thing. Our workshop *Tausend und eine Nacht* Corps 1047 (Arabian Nights) found just the opposite! This work came as a welcome change from the switchboards - peeling potatoes, swedes, and cutting cabbages. What were the dinners like? The password was "swede-cabbage", *kapusta* (cabbage) swedes or "swedes-cabbage". Nearly every Prussian hates this food. Sometimes, on Sundays, when we have saved potatoes, we get *Gulasch* (beef stew)!! or as yesterday, *Sauerkraut*, potatoes and beef. This is a welcome treat as to a traveller in the desert who is thirsty and finds water! and even more so, the jelly that follows. It is all well prepared, tastes jolly good, as good as at home. Quite often there are left-overs and the hungry get a huge second helping. First in the line is Rohr, then Volze and me as, of course, we are always hungry. When we make dumplings, we put some in our pockets and like jacket potatoes, they taste good for supper. With our rations we could exist if they gave us the correct amount of grammes, but those cook-house scoundrels! For three days we should have 1,800gr. bread, 165gr. fat, 100gr. sausage or cheese, 110gr. sugar, 185gr. jam, 30gr. tobacco, 4 cigars and 4 cigarettes. Quite often we get less. For example instead of 165gr. fat 120gr. or 70gr. sugar and the same amount of cheese or even 60gr. jam.

Despite stormy weather, 115 enemy aircraft were spotted and 39 shot down. The 20th-29th Nov. 1917 was the date of the tank battle of Cambrai. On the 20th, it began with heavy firing in the night. The next day, suddenly, at 8 a.m., a shell exploded with a loud bang. Three or four minutes later, when I went into the yard, where Wachtm. Schonber and our cook were standing, another exploded. In the course of the morning, Tommy delivered 8 shells. There was a lot of confusion. The British were trying to break through the lines. For this reason, a whole Division (the 2142D) arrived on the night of 21/22 as reinforcements. The headquarters was moved here and gave a lot of extra work with the telephone calls. Every time one came, either Hauptm. Perkuhn or Ritter von Pristwitz u. Gaffron (30 years old) had to be called. All the time there were carrier-pigeon messages from Infantry Regiment von Paczenski, sent 1 p.m. arrived 1.30 p.m.: "Last news, English infantry surrounding sugar factory, withdrawing. Night patrols against the southern edge of Bourlon Wood driven back. N.W. outskirts of Fontaine occupied by enemy machine-guns. Tanks rolling back and forth along the road from Bourlon Wood." Or, "Enemy attacking Marcoing with heavy forces. Reinforcements needed urgently. Machine-gun ammunition destroyed. Act quickly". Or, "23.11.17. Infantry Regiment 50, English have broken through 10/50 with tanks and infantry, immediate back-up needed". Or, "Infantry Reg. 50, Enemy break through Bourlon Wood with tanks. Some troops in retreat. Inf.Reg. 175 occupies railway embankment".

We were glad when the Infantry Division withdrew after a few days. During this time, shots were fired continually over our heads into neighbouring villages (4KM.) Aubencheul and Aubigny le Bac. There, the English were firing on the railway and canal. On 27th, they turned on us with 22 shots. At 12.30

a.m. the last one fell. Presumably, they were shells with a huge dispersal power, shot from a ship's cannon. It was terrifying when the shells exploded. Tommy wanted to bomb the Pioneers' stores. The shells fell mostly as far as the carrier-pigeon loft. So, for example, 7 shots spaced out at 15m. exactly behind each other. Shrapnel fell with a loud noise on our roof. Our group leader, who thought he was going to change duties any moment, slept in the Station during these critical days. On 28th, I had to take a message to the Pioneer Building because their cable was broken. But, luckily, the moon was shining brightly. Of course, in the Pioneer compound there was not a soul to be seen. It looked uncanny with the iron structures, wood and ammunition. Along the Front, flares flashed ever nearer. I ran hither and thither and almost lost my nerve, any moment Tommy could drop a bomb. At last, I found a Gefr. who wanted to go to the Pioneers, who were in a dug-out 10m deep. I was glad when I gave them the telephone message - someone wanted 18,000 hand grenades - and had left the yard behind. Hardly had I reached our quarters when a bomb fell. Then others flew over our heads. Shrapnel fell on our roof. Shortly after, another bomb fell, then all was quiet.

On 30th November, for two and a half hours, I watched, as I often did, the battle of Bourlon Wood which we could see clearly from our little hill. Numerous bombs exploded and in some places, one could see gaps in the forest (trees shot down). It was a haunting sight to see an aircraft fall in flames, probably a German one, unfortunately. It looked to us like a glowing piece of iron dropping to the ground. About 25 German aircraft flew constantly backwards and forwards. Some were there to protect the 7-8 air balloons. One English pilot tried to attack a balloon. This was immediately withdrawn. At the same time, 2 Revolver cannons attacked, whose green whistling cannonballs, at regular intervals, tried to hit the plane but it got away. I should have loved to have watched it all for hours. Twice I went forward to the German firing batteries, firing on Bourlon which lay on the other side of the road from Epinoy, Sanchy and Lestree.

During the last few days in November, Brandt and I decided to go to Baralle on the road from Arras to Cambrai but on 2nd December, we had to leave Oisey. I was sorry about this because the Cambrai battle was still going on. After a 4 hour march, which took us through Aubencheul, Aubigny an Bac, Fechan, Wasnes an Bac and Marquette, we arrived in Bouchain. In Aubencheul, Volze gave me a small sack of potatoes which were very welcome. Bouchain, a small fortress with 3,000 inhabitants, lies on a canal where there is a lot of activity. On the first day, we were nine men to a room. As there were no beds, we had to put our bedding on the floor - wonderful at this time of year! During the night of 3rd/4th December, the Officers' Mess, once a castle, went up in flames. I watched for a time then did not bother despite the fire alarms ringing. In all villages there are alarms (pieces of iron) which carry the inscription: "Seulement pour announcer l'incendie".

Soon, the first parcels arrived. From writing to the wife of the Councillor for Commerce, I received from Gunter Schleiper, Thorn, Schulstr. 9., a parcel with the following contents: a book, a pack of cards, Russian Drops, 30 cigarettes, Army postcards and a pencil. After that, I had a small parcel from Ruth (cousin) with sweets and a letter. Shortly after, another Christmas present - a cake and a whole Pommeranian sausage which, when we had little fat, was very welcome. Later, more and more parcels arrived from benefactors. The crowning present was a large parcel which Zabel, on leave, brought from home, with eggs, bacon, lard, and a large cake - a very acceptable present for a soldier's hungry stomach. During the run up to Christmas a choir practised carols when off duty. There were clergy, former actors, an excellent singer and a conductor.

All that we needed was a Christmas tree but where can we get one without stealing? One day, when I was on duty on the switchboard, a wagon with Christmas trees stopped just in front of the Station. After a few polite words, we were give not one but TWO trees. The celebration was a very simple wartime effort. A Christmas tree, with eleven candles, decorated the room to signify the importance of this Festival. Gunther opened the proceedings with a short address and then distributed 4 Iron Crosses 2nd Class and one Würtemberg Medal.

One day after Christmas, I went for a walk to Lourches. This place has 8,000 inhabitants and is a coal-mining town lived in, almost without exception, by coal-miners. One house looks like the next and everywhere is black with smoke. Several days later, we went along the canal via Steuville, from Lourches to Denam. Vogel, who draws very well (an architect), did several drawings and at the same time, showed me the art of drawing in perspective. In Denam, we found ourselves surrounded by workers' houses. There were the same "establishments" as in Lourches and on every window of the brothels a notice "Forces. No entry" - about 40 along one street! We wanted to go back when a comrade we met told us that the real town was in the opposite direction. There was a theatre and even a castle with a magnificent garden and we were cheeky enough to look into the front windows although it said "No Trespassers". Denam was about as big as Cambrai (26,000 inhabitants). Prices, as in other French towns, were very high. One Madame wanted 12M for 1lb. sugar, 24M for one metre of Alpaca, a pair of shoes 60M, 1 tablet soap 5.5M, a few cigarettes 1.50M.

For the last hours of the old year, we wanted to celebrate, despite the war and prepared tables with white cloths on which stood a small Christmas tree, left over from Christmas, Odol (mouth disinfectant) and Wuttki (Vodka Pol.) or Firewater. I, as youngest, wanted the older ones, 'the heroes', to have pride of place and myself disappear in a corner, but was commanded by Wachtm. Gunther to sit at his right-hand and play the part of 'Cupbearer'. Just as I was beginning to enjoy myself, I had to go on night duties. Midnight came nearer and nearer. I saw the year pass in front of my eyes like a film. Now midnight! Then 1918. Shots were fired and hurrahs shouted then everything went quiet.

At about 2 a.m., 8 comrades came into the Station and wished us a Happy New Year. One of the clerks, Rummert, even brought his fiddle with him. Now the fun started, all of them were merry, music, noise, Indian dances, etc. Then came the Goose March (one behind the other) and they went to the saw-mill, coming back at 4 a.m. after they had drunk 3 buckets of beer. They wanted to put Rummert, who had enjoyed too much beer, into a hero's coffin and carry him home. On the way, even his fiddle was damaged. In the meantime, all the sergeants came to wish us a Happy New Year. Only one, Wachtm. Matthieson, couldn't go any further and threw himself onto the bed but it was turned over and he was pelted with pillows. It was all good fun. Lots of others, who took part, offered good wishes and they all celebrated. How long did I have to listen to gramophone music through the telephone!! How glad I was when morning came.

On 2.1., I was relieved from switchboard duties and came to the Fault Repair Unit for training - to my advantage. That went quickly. With a belt, iron grips on the boots, and a portable telephone, I climbed the telegraph poles and blocks. On 4.1., an English 'plane appeared and dropped bombs on the railway station and disrupted a number of telephone wires. Nine men were killed. This caused a lot of work and soon we were relieved by two Construction Corps. What an immense power shrapnel has! One piece passed through the top of a rail two finger widths thick.

On the evening of the fifth, the Wachtm. called me and said that I had to do relief work and go either to Marquette

(Arras Group) or Paillencourt. The Chief of Staff was in Marquette but I wanted to have as little as possible to do with the High Command and all the work involved and so chose Paillencourt. There I came to the Fault Section. On 6.1.18 we are 3 men and an Untffr. The latter and I share a room. We three together do all the work but the Untffr. doesn't play his part. He spends his time eating, sleeping and praying but looks out for the smallest mistakes. Name, Behagel, an engineer of 40 years. His father is Councillor Dr. Behagel from Mannheim. Quite often there are no repairs but after a storm we have a lot to do. When the weather is damp, as it is now in January, it is no pleasure climbing cable poles. Clay is at home here, so to speak, and boots sink in up to the ankles. When we get back, our legs are unrecognisable blocks of clay. What a time it takes to clean them! Boots, shoes, jacket or coat, everything is smeared with mud.

On 13.1, a Sunday, I went for a walk to Cambrai, famous for its tank battle; a two hour walk via Thun Leveque, Eswas, Ramillies and Morenchies. The town, with 26,000 inhabitants, is surrounded by a high wall on the eastern side. A canal runs through the town. When I entered the town, I noticed the cellar openings were protected by stones and rubble. Out of every window came a pipe from a stove. These were the living quarters, the place of refuge during the shelling of the English troops. Even now, one saw one or two with smoke coming out, an indication that they were still living quarters. Like Lille, the town had not been badly hit. Only near the *jardin public*, where there was an undefended side, were the houses destroyed along a short street. The Market Square, with its *Hôtel de ville*, now army headquarters, made a favourable impression. Around midday, when people had been to church, the streets were crowded. The great majority of people were dressed in black. One of the sights was the cathedral built in MDCCCLXV (1865). It was beautiful from the outside as well as inside. The organ, as well as some art treasures, was protected by sandbags. It had a tower and on the golden crown stood the Saviour. Nearby is St. Gery Church. Part of the roof, damaged by a direct hit has fallen in. I climbed halfway up the tower and had a wonderful view of the town. There was a third church there with a spire similar to Strassburg Cathedral but entry was forbidden. In nearly all the churches, so far as I have seen, they have chairs instead of pews. During Holy Communion, for instance, by the Consecration, all the worshippers turn their chairs round so that the back can be used for supporting the elbows. All the churches are Romanesque. Opposite the cathedral is a *seminaire*. At first, I thought it was a riding school, or chapel of prayer. Whether it was a theological college or a teachers' training college, I don't know. It was probably the former but is now a cinema. Then I asked the way to the Park and looked at the monument to Bleriot. There is a monoplane chiselled into a globe. Underneath is written just "Afrique". Written on the base is "Louis Bleriot sa ville natale en commemoration de sa traversee de la Manche, le 25 juillet 1909". There are a great number of well designed barracks on the outskirts of the town. They now have German names: *Kürassier, Marewitz* and *Hindenburg* barracks. By chance, I met our new platoon commander, Dalibor from Silesia, who has served 17 years in the army. From the hill in Paillencourt, we can see Cambrai. When we were in Oisey, we could see it to the south.

On 13.1., we received belated presents. Everyone was given a bag. Mine had ¼ lb. bonbons, biscuits, sewing kit, note-paper, a bar of soap, 10 Swiss cigars and 20 cigarettes. On 18.1., a travelling theatre visited this place and of course, there were a large number of people who attended. Besides humorous speeches and poems, there were music-hall songs and drinks all round.

Up until now, we belonged to the Sixth Army with the same commander, now, we belong to the Second Army, under the command of General von der Marwitz. As well as this, we are in the XLV Reserve Corps which is divided into several groups. We belong to the Arras Group not the Reserve Group 5 but Group 15 which is based in Oberhofen in Alsace. On 26.1., the Arras Group announced that one from our Fault Section should go to Army headquarters, Warte, in Bourlon. Ka., who should have gone, was not very keen, so I volunteered to go. On 27.1., I was fetched in a hearse from Marquette. We drove via Thun Leveque and Eswas. There, we were given another car and drove on, via Ramillies and Morenohies, to Cambrai. From there we took the Cambrai-Arras road and left Fontaine to reach Bourlon.

There we came to the 10m. deep dug-out of the headquarters *Sachsenhausen* on the other side of the forest. The village of Bourlon is totally destroyed - a heap of rubble. Both of the castles and house walls are intact but riddled with holes. The interior of the church is devastated. Under the High Altar is a recess where there was probably once a coffin. Now there is just a scattering of human bones. From the red castle before the shellings ran a wide, once beautiful, avenue of trees. Now, $7/8$ of the forest is damaged, $3/4$ of the trees broken off. Everything lies in confusion. It is difficult to get to as English trenches run through the forest in which a number of weapons lie around. Puttees are very much sought after. I have counted 30 tanks in the village, the wood and round about. Now, at the end of February, the motors and inner parts are being taken out and sent back to Germany. The motors are Daimler 105 H.P. The tanks are not all the same size. Above are two laths on which a thick beam with reinforcements can be moved and used under the tank when it cannot move forward. Each track moves separately. It turns when one track moves and the other is stationary. It is manned by one officer and 8 men, who are said to be paid 1,000M per month. One finds scattered human remains - a hand, a leg.

When the weather is good, the view from here is magnificent. With the naked eye, one can see the Cambrai-Arras road in the area around Marquion, Inchy, Nivenores, Graincourt, Havrincourt and the forest of Havrincourt where the English Artillery is stationed, yes, even Hermies, which is 10Km. away. With the steriotelescope one can see as far as Lagnicourt, Louveral, Boursies, Beaumetz and Denincourt. One can also see the Front which runs through Graincourt, Nivenores and Inchy and further where it runs through Pronville, Onicent and Riencourt. These places are still under our control. Very often alarm signals are given. On 16.2., an English assault was expected but except for some skirmishes, nothing happened. Our Front line lies, in part, 3Kms from our look out. Our dug-out is large and built with two exits. There are nine rooms. In the largest, there are 6 men, plus our cookhouse. Now that we have a self-made "Family Table" it is more comfortable. Of course, it is always dark. A Carbide lamp is all we need but when the fuel runs out, we have to sit in the dark but this does not happen very often. The diet is poor although one has the 750gr. bread of the fighting troops to help satisfy one's hunger. If I hadn't been issued with a large tin of meat when rations were given out, I would have almost starved. The midday meal is very watery and then only one and a quarter litres. However, the parcels that come from home are a great help.

On the evening of 14.2., came the news that an armistice had been signed with Russia. Here, in the dug-out, on 14.2., I celebrated my 19th birthday without anyone knowing about it. The large number of letters that I had received was the only celebration. The post is fetched every three days from Blécourt. There, on 13.2., I met Kippler and Jablonski, two fellow sufferers from the garrison in Hammerstein. Both had been awarded the Iron Cross 2nd Class as a token of distinction in the Fault Section during the battle of Cambrai. We were overjoyed to see each other again.

On 19.2., two of us went to the Front line, with a camera, to take a photograph of an aircraft which lay between Bourlon and Inchy. Not far away, English shells fell one after the other. Suddenly 3 shells and in a flash, we stuck our heads almost in the clay. Hundreds of pieces of shrapnel flew around so we decided to get up and disappear.

In Steinbruchwald, we found shell holes almost the size of rooms. The artillery was active and it was unpleasant when the shells fell in the vicinity. In the dug-out entrance, I could stand safely and hear the noise of the shrapnel. The other day, in the village, I saw a vehicle that I had never seen in my life before - a motorised vehicle for dragging away the English tanks and which itself had a track like the English tanks and turned by moving only one. Up until now, Tommy had only once used gas grenades. At first, it smelt like fresh apples. If one breathed in a little, the eyes water but with more it could be life threatening. Everyone quickly fetched his gas mask. Even in the bunker you could smell it. On 7.3., I went for a walk to Fontaine, on the Cambrai-Bapaume road. One notices the spring weather here and the sunshine is very pleasant. For this reason life improves from day to day.

Shortly before the offensive on 10th March, we were relieved by the Tel.Unit of 53. Reserve Division. We went to the switchboards which were moved, in the meantime, to Hayncourt. The village was full of troops. The first two nights, we slept in a half ruined clay hut. Then we were moved into a small castle where we were given a very large room for eleven men, our office and apparatus: we were packed like herrings. Our house is surrounded by a beautiful garden. Already, in the middle of March, there are flowering cherries, laurel and apricots. On 9.3, in the Bourlon Wood, on a sunny slope, are white anemones. On 10th March, I was in Cambrai, for the fourth time, in order to get rid of lice. In this place, one has to give up all one's clothes, have a hot bath, while the clothes are put into a hot room. When one has finished washing, the clothes are given back. Stoller, who spent three months on the Front, is now Gefr.. The Tel. Sec. is a step behind.

The big offensive is now ready. All the villages near the Front are full of troops. Troop movement is on a massive scale, all roads leading to the Front have been repaired. Everywhere, one sees that things are going to happen in the next few days. Yesterday, we were issued with steel helmets. At last, we have got rid of the *Tschakos* (caps.Pol.) and are proper soldiers. On 15.3, four of us, Gefr. Gutjahr, Stations Ältester Brechauer, Peters and I took 20 minutes to get through the straggling village of Laurcourt to take over the Tel. Station. This is in a dug-out. Although there are no civilians, the place is very busy. With so many soldiers here, they have to sleep outside. Absolutely everywhere is crammed with troops.

What would be an interesting spectacle is the huge gun standing in the park. It is a 38cm. barrel but unfortunately, we are not allowed near it. Our quarters are in a nice big room. Enemy planes are constantly on the move, a sign that the offensive will soon begin and rumour has it that this should begin on 19.3. Our 38cm. will also make a bit of noise! A day later, 21.3.18, was the great day. From 4 a.m. column after column of snipers etc. marched towards the Front. At 5.10 a.m. there was a devastating bang! The first shot was fired. A huge fireball lit up the sky - a 14cwt shell. It flew towards Bapaume. 4cwt gunpowder is needed for one shot, and it travels 54Kms. The English Headquarters in Bapaume is under attack as well as other places. With us, all quarters within a radius of 400m have to be evacuated. We, too, were without a roof over our heads. As everywhere was occupied, we moved back into our place where all the windows had been blasted out and even bits of wall had fallen down. At every shot, we thought the place was going to collapse. A shot was fired every 7, then every 3, minutes. But after several had been fired, we heard that there had been an accident. The gun had been partly destroyed and 4 men killed and 12 wounded. The 38cm. was silent.

On 25.3., we returned to our Company in Haynecourt. There our worn clothing was replaced. I was given a new pair of trousers. On 26.3., at 1 p.m. the march forward began via Bourlon, the road to Anneux and then the main Cambrai-Bapaume road was the route we followed. Behind the sugar factory in Graincourt, on the canal, was the first English position. Then came Boursies. Even before that we halted for a rest. Along the road to the trenches was a pipe taking water. Further on, we saw the remains of a German plane, still in good shape. Underneath lay the pilot with just underpants. All along the road were dead soldiers - up to Bengny nearly all our soldiers, after that those of the English. In the ditches along the road these unfortunate souls are lying, their faces covered by a thick layer of dust, the head bent slightly forward, crouching, some still with their back packs and helmets. Nearly all of them had the shoes or boots taken away and their packs rifled looking for valuables.

At 7 p.m., we arrived in Bengny, our goal. Away from the village, we found shelter in dug-outs which had been used by the English. These were half in the ground and the upper half covered with corrugated iron and sandbags round the sides. Of course, it was not very warm. In our free time, we wandered round the fields and found dead bodies everywhere with weapons and clothing especially blankets and trench coats which we put on. Some of the bodies looked ghastly. For example, a German soldier whose eyes and cheeks had been gnawed by rats. Others were naked, others with broken skulls. A lot of clothing, which had been removed, lay strewn around. I could have done with another pair of underpants.

Edwin Kühns and Walter Baum at the Training Camp Hammerstein.
23.8.1917. Leaving for the Front.

Telephone Operators in the Field Exchange and at the Front.

Mobile carrier pidgeon loft. (Q29950)

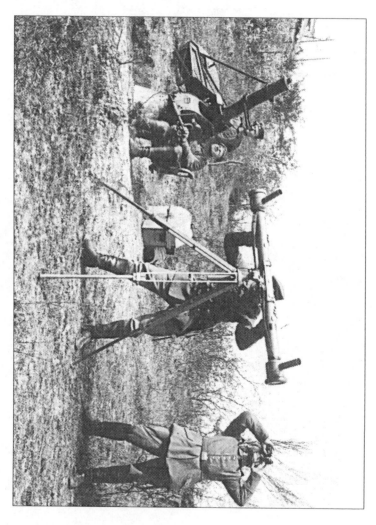

A stereoscopic telescope.

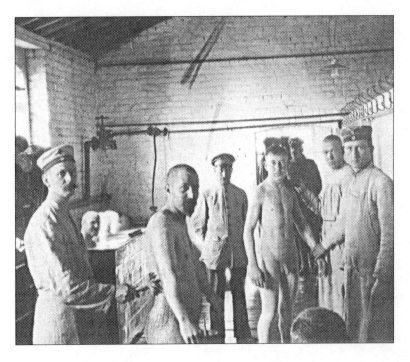

In the de-lousing Sanitary Station.

Battle of Cambrai. British tanks with fascines.

Troops massing in a small town ready for the Offensive.

Papa Bruno Kühns.
(1872 - 1945).
In charge of a
Field Food Depot.

The Cambrai Sector under General George von der Marwitz (Headquarters in Spa) was a quiet area known as 'Flander's Sanatorium' where tired Divisions and wounded were sent.

*German baggage-wagons retreating through Belgium in November 1918.
The vehicles halted in this small town-square represent a typical selection of
army transport, a few motor vehicles but the majority horsedrawn; the crews
mostly wear the comfortable soft cap (Mutze) in preference to the helmet.
The smoke rises from a portable field kitchen, a wheeled vehicle with a fire
which could be kept burning on the march. From its chimney, which was
stowed horizontally for transportation and which gave the appearance of a
gun barrel, the vehicle was commonly styled a Gulasch-kanone ('stew-gun').*

Edwin Kühns

ORGANIZATIONAL TABLES:
GERMAN ARMY, 1914

Although each army organized its forces in its own national methods, a number of similarities existed, in that it was usual for an Army Corps to be a completely self-contained entity with all necessary supporting services attached to the Corps, rather than to a central depot from which the necessary support units were drawn as required.

The following tables are typical, demonstrating the usual organization of the German Army in 1914, after mobilization. The most significant change between the pre-war and mobilization organization of a German Corps was that it was usual for the cavalry brigades to be withdrawn from the divisional organization and formed into independent Cavalry Divisions, leaving only a small cavalry contingent attached at infantry divisional level as a reconnaissance force. (The Order-of-Battle of II Corps above includes the pre-war disposition of cavalry with the infantry divisions).

A typical Army Corps upon mobilization was organized as follows:

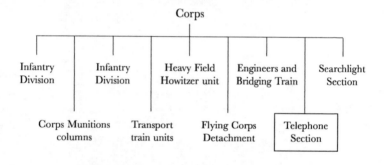

Divisional establishment in 1914 was:

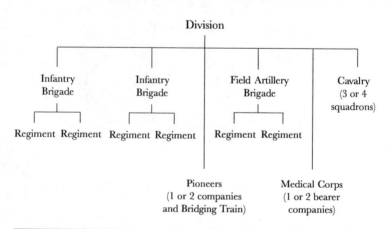

An infantry regiment in 1914 was organized in three battalions, with companies numbered consecutively from 1 to 12, with the separate machine-gun company (not attached to a battalion) numbered 13.

On 27.3., seven of us, after we had been split into groups, marched from the Company - Untffr. Lemien was in charge. We should have gone to Puisieux but the English were there, so we marched at first to Bapaume, where we had to find protection from the enemy planes. The west of Bapaume is in ruins but I do not know what the rest of it looked like, I could not see in the dark. By nightfall, we had reach Grévillers and looked for night quarters. Yesterday, our troops had taken Achiet, so it said in the despatches 26.3. Here, for the time being, we should establish an Intelligence Station. As it was a long way from the town, we transferred our quarters, which is a corrugated iron shed, 1Km. away. Many of the troops who came later, envied us and rightly so. It is no joke, during the rainy spells, to have to live without a roof over your head. Easter came ever nearer. On Good Friday, it rained the whole day. At this time, the food got worse. On Easter Sunday, we had nothing except half a loaf of bread per man. We were inconsolable. Everyone was miserable as they were so hungry. A comrade brought a joint of horsemeat from a horse that had been killed, which we had to roast but everyone had only about ¼ lb. That was the first horsemeat that I had knowingly eaten. It was very tough but tasted good. The day was very dull and windy. I often thought about the lovely roast that they were probably having at home. I was aware that we had a number of slightly wounded soldiers amongst us. Every day when we were still in Sancourt, whole Divisions marched through.

5.4., we are still in Grévillers. Our Intelligence Station has now become an exchange. 12 men work in pairs on a field switchboard with 20,10,5 cables. Yesterday, we heard that on 5.4. there would be a second offensive. At 5 a.m. our Artillery fired gas. 8 a.m., the Infantry went forward. As yet we do not know the outcome. During the last days, I heard that Papa was in Hautmont near Maubeuge - still 50Km. from Cambrai and 80Km. from where we are in Grévillers. Perhaps by chance, we could meet. Papa came with a Motorised Division to Orignies near St. Quentin. I set my mind on going there, but the Ltn. thought it would take over a week under these conditions, so I gave up. On several occasions I tried to 'phone Papa. During the day it was difficult. At night, I managed to get through to the depot but the sleeping quarters were elsewhere. The connection as far as Guise was poor, to Orignies almost impossible. On 11.4., the English shelled Grévillers. I was on duty outside the drivers' quarters when, behind the house, about 25m. away, an unexploded bomb fell. If it had gone off, I wouldn't be sitting here. They were probably 18 or 24 pounders. Yesterday I counted 22 German balloons on the horizon. On 17.4., 2 a.m., an almighty bang shook our quarters. Mysteriously, everything lurched together. A shell fell in our midst and we scattered in every direction. A shelter, not far away, gave us enough protection for those from our quarters. In the space of one or two seconds, shells crashed down, ten altogether. The damage was far reaching. Both motor vehicles from the Transmission Station and several army huts were destroyed. The one on duty in the former was killed. The Tel. Operator, who was reading the daily bulletin, had his head almost blown off. 8 were dead. 30 wounded. Five horses were also killed. During the next few days, the food improved - the meat ration was bigger! Horse meat is rather tough but everyone liked it, even those who would not have eaten it if they had known beforehand. The next day, most of the army huts were evacuated; we would have to move in the next few days. Our quarters received two pieces of shrapnel. For more than a fortnight, we have had proper April weather - rainy and cool. Today, even in the morning, there was hail and a thin layer of ice on the water in the shell holes. We don't like the food. *Drahtverhau* (spaghetti) and *sauerkraut* are the daily rations. On 20.4., we moved to the Bapaume-Albert, Grévillers-Thilly crossroads. The day before, we had to build our own quarters.

The station was a cement construction with 1m. thick walls built by the English which gave protection from grenades and bomb splinters. There was a good deal of work covering it with earth. It was hard work, too, as not only was it clay, but already a spade deep was water.

On 28.4., three men, including myself, were transferred to the Long Distance Transmission in Lausitz, which lay in a wood west of Grév. Our place is a real convalescent home. Five men, an Untffr. and one Ltn. are in one hut. The whole floor of the woodland is covered with violets, anemones and marsh marigolds, bluebells and other flowers in full bloom. One can do what one likes. I am the cook and up till now, everything has turned out well. The quality is left to be desired. Stoller has been granted 3 months leave for school purposes. On 3rd May, I asked Wachtm. Dalibor if I could be granted leave to visit Papa. On 4.5., at 7.30 a.m. I set off with a cycle. The route went via Bapaume and Péronne. The latter is better preserved than Bapaume and lies in the valley of the Somme. From there I went via Athies where I was given a good meal by the Tel. Sec. there, consisting of meat and noodles, before continuing to Ham. In Croix Moligneau I 'phoned the depot in Villers St. Christophe where I hoped to meet my father. There, I was given the bad news that Papa was now in Chevresie Monceau near La Perté south-east of St. Quentin.

I was in two minds about going back as it was already 3 p.m. Papa, to whom I spoke by telephone, said that I should continue and I rode on to Ham. There I was lucky enough to meet the driver of a lorry which was going to St. Quentin so I hung onto the back of it. The last named town had formerly 55,000 inhabitants but now it was severely damaged. There was barbed wire through the centre of the town. The beautiful cathedral was partly demolished. Now I had to go via Neuville and Harcourt to Mezieres on the Oise. It was a terribly bad path which went over the trenches. Mezieres was beautifully situated. Then came Surfontaine and Tay le Noyer. I had to ride along cart tracks and I had no map. The sun had disappeared a long time ago. Tears came into my eyes through desperation but at last, I arrived, at 11 p.m. in absolute darkness, in Chevresie, dead tired. Papa stood, in a white jacket, in front of the door and called my name as I gave a ring on my bell from time to time.

We were very happy and went to bed very late. Unfortunately, the next morning he had to be on duty from 7 a.m.-noon and 2 p.m. to 6 p.m. I was able to satisfy a very hungry stomach with liver sausage, brown stew, butter and sugar. There were stacks of everything. I was able to stay two whole days. On the 6th, I began to pack my things and of course, took a good supply of food with me. It was so enjoyable that I didn't want to leave. On 7th, it began to rain in the morning but I had to go. I had already overstepped my leave by a day. I left at 7.20 a.m. and was hardly 10 minutes on the way when my coat slipped off, so I had to turn back. Then I rode via Parpeville, Pleine Selve and Ribemont to Origny. Here again, I found a lorry going in my direction but several Kms. before St. Quentin it broke down. Because the main road to St. Quentin was blocked I had to make a detour to get there. I arrived at 1 p.m. and then rode further on via Holnon to Vermand, the old Roman road and turned off before Estrees en Chaussee to Pervane and arrived at 9.15 p.m. in Grévillers. The journey there had been 115Km. compared to 95Km on the way back.

I didn't get back to my old duties on the long-distance calls in Lausitz and am now back in the Fault Section. Up until 23.6., I was on the switchboard. During this time, there were often differences of opinion between myself and the Stations Ältester, Behagel. In order to avoid further confrontation, Watchtm. Dalibor sent me to relieve Untffr. Vogel in Michael Camp which was on the road Bengy-Haplicourt. Here, we have 12 connections between 3 men. The Station and Quarters are in one room. There are hardly any duties. In May, Ruth (cousin) wrote that her brother, Walter, had been killed on 24th April on the Western Front. He was only 21 years of age and as a minethrower, was in the 112th Infantry Regiment.

Some days ago, six men were transferred from our platoon. Rohr and H. to the Infantry and 4 to the Field Artillery. Now ten more of those under 35 years of age, including me, will be called up. We are expected to be transferred in July. For me it is not a happy prospect as the younger ones are picked for the Storm Troops. Now an obstacle has been put in the way of my home leave. Should I be able to go, then Papa must come too. On 21.6., I was able to talk to Papa personally for the first time. Until then, either I couldn't get through or it was impossible to hear properly. Through 14 R.K. group Berg, A.O.K.2, A.O.K.18 Ham, I was able to get through to the Assembly Point for the wounded and sick and from there to Quarter Master Papa Kühns. I was very happy with this. Leave prospects: Friday 26.7. should be the departure date. Now it is Thursday evening and the papers have still not come through. No doubt I shall have to wait until the following Friday. Papa left on the 24th. I am devastated.

At the moment, I am with the Fault Section. There is a lot of work to do, for example, yesterday, from 6.30 a.m. to 8 p.m., we had nothing to eat except breakfast as we were working on the Aerial Defence cable as far as Courcelette, 7Km away. Near Sars are more tanks. If only the papers for my home leave would come! And they did! Departure: 1st August. On 2.8., I left Velu at 3.28 p.m. It just poured with rain. Thank goodness I had sent my *Affen* (monkey), i.e. my pack, the day before with the provisions' cart to Bengy. From there, Wachtm. Witt drove me to Velu. I arrived at the station wet to the skin although I was wearing my coat. With me was the horse driver Kr. From Briesen who, in August 1917, belonged to my group from Hammerstein.

At 8 p.m., the feeder train brought us to the collecting station. Here, we had our first meal which was noodles and meat. Then we were divided into separate carriages and at 3.48 a.m. MU219 began to move in the direction of Germany. Alone with my comrades, I sat in a 3rd class compartment as far as Thorn. During the night we slept very well. The train was hardly half full. The journey went via Cambrai, Douai, Wallers, through Belgium, Aachen, Cologne, Düsseldorf, Hagen, Soest, Paderborn, Holzminden and Seesen. It was Sunday evening when some day-trippers, young girls with mandolins, were standing on the platform. The train remained a long time in the station, as at every major station, where we got out.

For a short time, we forgot the serious side of life and there was laughter, rejoicing and chatter which I shall never forget as long as I live. The area around the Harz Mountains is very beautiful with deciduous forests, hills, little streams and tunnels 1000m. long . Further on we passed Halberdstadt, Magdeburg, Finsterwalde, Kottbus - it was here that the first men left the train - Guben, Bentschen, Posen and Hohensalza, finally arriving in Thorn. Everyone was here to meet us. In Hohensalza, I put on my puttees to make a good impression.

Until 11.8., Papa and I were there together. The days spent in Thorn were wonderful but the time went so quickly. Visiting all my friends took a long time. During the 14 months that I had been away, boys and girls had grown a head taller. There are very few young men about. One sees only invalids, those not fit enough for military service or war disabled. It is only with these that the girls can flirt as other men are hard to come by. On the last day of my leave, Christik is buried. The poor chap died of consumption and was only 20 years old. Talaska and the consumptive Garske were there too. Following my idea, they bought a wreath too.

We ate very well at home. I brought 3 loaves of bread and Papa brought 2 from the depot; then, before my departure, I fetched two more which the Inf. Regiment gave me because I was going back to the Western Front!

Thursday, 1.30 a.m., I have to leave for at least another year. Oh, this interminable time! We arrived by train on 26.8. What a change! Already in Cambrai I learnt, by 'phone, that we were no longer in Grévillers. As I asked for the Unit Gera, I was told that the Tommies were there. In Pelu, I met the Platoon 16 R.D. Today, 27.8.18., the English have occupied the first houses in Bapaume. Our old cement block had suffered a direct hit. From a Brigade who occupied it after we left, 4 men were killed. Everything is the same as the forward march in March this year only in the reverse direction but there is no hurry. Everyone is camping in the open. Only Division 7 is in operation, the others have been disbanded. We have established our station with the 44 Infantry Division. A multi-switchboard is in operation and from today, I am working on it as well. It works like the Post Office switchboard, with the difference that one can serve 150 from one board. When a latch is engaged, it makes a crackle when one puts in the plug. In our hut we have a true saying:

Stopsel hin, Stopsel her,	Plug here, Plug there,
Stopsel kreuz, Stopsel quer	Plug crossed, Plug away,
Stopsel richtig, sei bedacht	Plug right, think again,
3 Tage sind schnell eingebracht	3 days in detention is easily earned.

On the morning of 29.8., we moved to Havrincourt because the air in Velu "had too much iron". We stayed here until 3.9. I had often looked through the stereotelescope toward Havrincourt from the observation post in Bourlon Wood. Our Exchange was outside the town, hidden in sloping ground. Not far away, there was a chapel, with a tomb of the Graf (Earl) of Havrincourt, underneath which was now a dug-out. There were a lot of passages. Built in one recess was the coffin of the Marquis. In the one on the opposite side, the coffin had been taken out and someone had tried to open it. It stood at an angle against the wall with an oak panel damaged and part of the zinc cover torn away. Underneath was a wooden board which had been bored into.

On the morning of 3.9., at 1.30 a.m., we moved from Havrincourt because by 2.30 a.m. we should have moved back our position. Unhindered by aircraft, we marched via Fleigmeres, Marcoing, Cambrai, Escandoevres and arrived, at 10 a.m., in Ivony. Everyone was overjoyed when we arrived, as since the end of March, we had been in the devastated Somme region where we saw neither house nor trees and lived in huts, dug-outs and shell-holes; the loneliness was getting unbearable. Here we would be happy to spend the winter. The main attractions were: there are civilians, a cinema, a soldiers' recreation centre and an Army bookshop. Quarters are magnificent. With three comrades, I live in a large room on the ground floor with a view towards the street. For our comfort, there is also electric light. The Station is in the house as well as the cookhouse. The former is in the cellar. We often go for walks to look around for pretty girls.

I have been able to 'phone several times to Papa, who is in Bohain, only 30Km. away. Yesterday Wachtm. Dalibor was promoted to Sub. Ltn. In the meantime, Papa has been transferred to Maubeuge where I spoke to him on 18.9. The connection was made via Solesmes, Avesnes but a better way is via Avesnes le Sec, Valenciennes. Papa says that he had marvellous quarters and no disturbance from aircraft. Shortly afterwards, Feldwebel. Lang's friend telephoned. His "Isegrim" Infantry Regiment 172 is now in Fressain. Not long ago, I received the sad news that Leo Rastankovski was missing and Alfons R. killed. May they be remembered.

After a long time, I received a letter from Walter (lifelong friend). They are now on the Vesle after he took part in the offensive near Chateau Thierry and now in the retreat. He was hardly back from leave when he had to take up his position receiving enemy information on the front line. "You have to keep up your courage. The old God still lives. In the terror of the war, my ideals and literature keep me going. Greetings and handshake! I wonder whether we shall ever shake hands again. May God give us the opportunity! Wonderful leave. I often think about you. 16 days of happiness at home were a compensation for the long winter." On 27.9., the civilians were evacuated. Tommy bombarded the ammunition dump there. A lot of nice things were left behind for us. Many of the cellars were full of potatoes. In warehouses and stores a lot was left behind. In our Station, we could buy as much honey as we wanted, 100 litres of beer, and 50 bags of rusks.

On 30.9., G. Meyer and my little self came to Solesmes, east of Cambrai, a town of 5,000 inhabitants, to get used to working with the Fault Section. Papa sent a telegram to say that he was with the Reserve Company in Hannan. The Platoon was in Sankoir. What we were supposed to do in Solesmes, no one knew. Our main thoughts were about food. As we were given double rations for several days, we had enough to eat. Quite often we made fried potatoes, once even semolina, with dried fruit sauce, as pudding. Quarters were not very good at the beginning, just a small attic. Later, I managed to reserve a nice furnished sitting room for us all.

On 7.10., our days were up. We were in retreat. We had to take over 3 Stations: Warignis le Grand, St. Waast and Roisin 28Km. via Romeries, Beaudignes, Le Quesnoy, Jeulein and Warignis le Grand. Gollert and myself manned the little exchange in Roisin, a village just behind the Belgian frontier. It is very quiet here, no troops, no danger of aircraft because this place lies in a quiet area between Valenciennes and Maubeuge

(20Km. away). The soldiers' leisure centre, with piano and harmonium as well as newspapers is the chief attraction in one's leisure time. Everything is well kept. There are two German nurses in charge.

Our Station has 8 lines of which 4 are out of order. Our Quarters are in the same house. The spaciousness makes a grand impression. Our house seems as though it was the Mayor's residence. We were just days here when one formation after another arrived until, in the end, the village was overflowing. As well as these, there were refugees with carts and wagons etc. The market square was full of them and they had to remain for the night. Many of them came from a long way away and were discharged from their transport and stayed. Many died. Our house was taken over by the Field Hospital 53. Now our quarters have to be in the same room as the Station. This is more convenient and comfortable but they would like our Tel.Sec. to take the poles under our arm and the switchboard on our shoulders and make room for, them but that wasn't to be.

For many hours I stood in G-Ward and saw the slaughter. The Tommies were treated harsher than our own men. Ruthlessly the surgeon pushed an instrument deep into the wound in order to make it smaller. On 18.10., 2.50 a.m., I tried to ring Alfons Dickman (lifelong school friend), after I had failed several times. Via Bellignes, Mons, Brussels and Cologne I managed to get Metz, from there Bonfontaine, Flackbattery 582, Scherszug 750, whose operator I had to thank for getting me through to Army Section Ruppert in Mons, where the clerk could only give me the bad news that Alfons had gone on duty. Perhaps I will try again. On 25th Oct., we strolled to Frameries and the next day, with Gollert from Minden and Untffr. Kallmbach, to Roeulx. Until November, we lived very comfortably. Our elderly landlady, a grandmother, looked after us soldiers very well. We never had to drink black coffee. Quite often, we had potatoes for supper and she even gave us her own butter. I didn't get bored on the switchboard as I often used to talk, for a long time, to the telephone operator in Sanke, a Miss Grote from Rixdorf.

On 6.11., we were in Rixdorf and on 9.11. we moved further on as the Platoon left the day before. Gollert and I and the garrison from Mons and Havré were ordered to march 45Km. to Ottignis. About 10 a.m., we started off. On the way we lost our two wagons with our packs, near Nivelles. Tired beyond words, we lay down against a straw stack in an open field to sleep. At midnight, after we had slept 3 hours in the straw, we marched on. It was bitterly cold and some of us had no coats or gloves. Later we slept another hour in a cowshed belonging to a sugar factory. At last, we arrived in Ottignis at 10 a.m. Here we took over the Exchange of the Army Headquarters. After we had reduced our belongings and loaded them, we marched on 13.11. to Wavre, 15.11. Gr. Rosiers, 16.11. Lens St. Remy, 17.11. Chokier on the Maas, and on 18.11. to Fraipont. I was put in charge of finding quarters for our platoon as well as the 1186, from Ottignis to Roetgen. As far as Lens St. Remy, Kallenbach and I rode on cycles, then as far as Fraipont, with others with the same task from the Army Headquarters, we drove in a personnel car. It was difficult to find anywhere for our men.

The P.O.W.s, who had been released, were given a welcome by the Belgians. In nearly every home I saw the same scene: English and French soldiers having breakfast with the family. They gave for an answer, "Toute est rempli". Quite often, they removed the stoves from our rooms and the best quarters that I could find were with a stone floor and 4 bare walls. On 13.11., we drove to Bachlen, near Limburg and those of us looking for quarters rode further on by cycle.

At 2 p.m., we happily crossed the German frontier which we had been looking forward to. Here we passed under the first banners, "Welcome to you soldiers now back on German soil". In Roetgen, near Eupen, near Aachen, we made our first rest in a German village. In our honour, they had put out flags. On some houses there were up to ten of them. The Belgians were greatly relieved to see the *Bosches* leave their borders. In our country we would be well received. Some people wanted to give us the last of what they had but we could not accept it. Provisions proved a difficulty. Fortunately, in Ottignis, we had furnished ourselves with flour, sugar and buckets of honey, otherwise we would have been very hungry.

In Wavre, we sold the things we no longer needed, firstly Gutjahr and then I, took over the bartering with the Belgians who did not want to pay very much. One chair we offered for 2M, later they only gave us IM. For an Army uniform 25M. For a good pair of boots they did not want to pay 25M. They offered 4-6M. for our blankets. They would not buy our telephone apparatus, worth 400M, for 50M. Switchboards, valued at 8-10,000M, we left behind. Anything valuable had to be destroyed. There was no possibility of taking them with us but we managed to make 200M.

On 21.11., we arrived at Niddegen. I and four others were lodged with a farmer who had four daughters. We enjoyed our evening with the family. I had the honour of sharing the sofa with the youngest daughter, 18 years old. For the night they made beds ready for us and the girls slept on straw in the kitchen. That was done without our knowing, otherwise we would not have taken their beds. Finding accommodation was a thankless task so Untffr. Kallenbach and I gave it up.

On 22.11., we arrived in Konradsheim near Lechenich. I took over the Exchange at the Army Headquarters, while the three others worked at the Post Office with three women operators. I would have liked to have been there too! Oh, what a pity! On 22.11., 7 a.m., I 'phoned Thorn via Cologne, Berlin. As it was a poor line, I gave it up but about half an hour later the operator in Thorn rang back and said he would like to speak to me. Again I dialled 669 and Mama came to the 'phone. Berlin intervened and I was told that Papa had already been discharged. On 23.11., I 'phoned Hindenburg (Upper Silesia) to speak to Ruth (cousin). There was no one at the Post Office as it was about midnight.

On 26.11., we left Konradsheim and marched to Bendsberg. Here on command of the Division, I was promoted to the rank of Gefr. as from 25.11. On 27.11., we managed to get to Wipperfurth, 28.11., to Ludenscheidt. From village to village we were accompanied by a happy bunch of children. On 29.11 we left at 4 a.m. We lost our way and arrived, 5 p.m., in Minden. We had marched almost 60Km. On 30.11 we arrived in Soest, near Paderborn. At last, we had reached our destination! So from France, through Belgium to Germany we marched 500 Km. We were housed in huge barracks. The younger ones amongst us should have been transferred to a Division, the rest to Ohrdruf (Thuringia) to the Reserve Unit in order to be discharged from there. The men were not satisfied with this and an Army Tribunal ruled that they should be discharged from Soest.

On 4.12., all those from the years 1896-99 were to be put together in a Tel.Sec. Platoon. On the same day, permission was given for half to go on leave, including myself. At 3.30 a.m. I set off by train for Hamm, and changed there to the Cologne-Berlin Express arriving in Charlottenburg at 3 a.m. having travelled 2nd class. Then I took the express to Eydkulmen and arrived in Thorn at 4.35 a.m. All the others from Thorn were already there. From Lechenich near Cologne, on 25.11, I rang Hidenburg (Upper Silesia). Because of the poor connection I just sent greetings to cousin Ruth. I thought that I would be the first back in Thorn but I was mistaken - most of my friends were already there.

The 14 days were soon gone. Many tried to persuade me to stay a few days longer for the Christmas celebrations. But I wanted to go back to Soest, where we were in private accommodation, as I was anxious to see the famous buildings of this old Hanseatic city but also to keep the friendship I had made with the young girls. The duties were pleasant too at both the Post Office and the Field Exchange and this made me want to return. Even pressure, particularly from my parents, did not persuade me to extend my leave. On one of the last days of my leave, I was informed, by chance, by a friend, Untffr. Pidman, that those of us in the first year at the Training College, when we had served our time in the Army, could be discharged. Because this affected me I went to the local Army Headquarters and asked to be transferred to a local Regiment in Thorn. I was transferred to the 4b Komp. Infantry Regiment 61 Reserve Battaltion and on 24.11.1918, properly discharged. What will my comrades in Soest have thought when not only I but two others on leave never returned?

On 3 Jan., 1919, I went back to the Training College and was put in the first year Group B working with Group A in the second year.